Minimalist Living for Peace of Mind

How to Appreciate the Simple Life

By: Patricia Foster

PUBLISHERS NOTES

Disclaimer

This publication is intended to provide helpful and informative material. It is not intended to diagnose, treat, cure, or prevent any health problem or condition, nor is intended to replace the advice of a physician. No action should be taken solely on the contents of this book. Always consult your physician or qualified health-care professional on any matters regarding your health and before adopting any suggestions in this book or drawing inferences from it.

The author and publisher specifically disclaim all responsibility for any liability, loss or risk, personal or otherwise, which is incurred as a consequence, directly or indirectly, from the use or application of any contents of this book.

Any and all product names referenced within this book are the trademarks of their respective owners. None of these owners have sponsored, authorized, endorsed, or approved this book.

Always read all information provided by the manufacturers' product labels before using their products. The author and publisher are not responsible for claims made by manufacturers.

Paperback Edition

Manufactured in the United States of America

Patricia Foster

DEDICATION

I would like to dedicate this to all frugals that want to live the Minimalist lifestyle and to be able to enjoy the tremendous benefits of leading this type of lifestyle.

> *"If saving money is wrong, I don't want to be right!"*

William Shatner

Minimalist Living for Peace of Mind

TABLE OF CONTENTS

Publishers Notes	2
Dedication	3
Chapter 1- Starting At New Home With The Minimalist Lifestyle	5
Chapter 2- The Minimalist Diet Plan	8
Chapter 3- Making The Transition To the Minimalist Lifestyle	11
Chapter 4- Simple Frugal and Minimalist Tactics	15
Chapter 5- Being Minimalist At The Office	19
Chapter 6- From The Office To The Home With Minimalism	23
Chapter 7- Minimalism For Students	26
Chapter 8- Tips For The Minimalist Traveler	30
Chapter 9- Back To Decorating Your Minimalist Style Home	33
About The Author	36

Patricia Foster

Chapter 1 - Starting At New Home With The Minimalist Lifestyle

Moving into a previously owned home can be a bit jarring. You are now moving into a structure that absorbed the character of the previous owners. Depending on whom you purchased the home from, you will have a great deal of work to do before the home will feel like yours.

Be careful!

Many new home owners begin to list all the things they would like to alter in their newly acquired home. Not only is this expensive, it is mentally exhausting. Rather than take on the entire home, you need to prioritize. Here are some simple and relatively inexpensive things to do to make that home feel like yours in no time.

Minimalist Living for Peace of Mind

First and foremost, give the house a good top to bottom scrubbing. The previous homeowners may have been lovely people, but chances are good that the home was neglected a bit in the cleanliness department. Fixtures, floors, refrigerator, lint screens of dryers, stairs, and carpets should all get your tender loving care. Tiles in the kitchen may need some extra attention, particularly the grout.

Use a simple cleaner and add some non-chlorinated bleach alternative to warm water. Let it soak on your grout and then scrub with a brush. Wipe, dry, and repeat until that tile looks like new! Windows will need to wiped, carpets may have to be steamed, and floors will need to be mopped. It will take much energy and sweat, but the result will be a sparkling clean home - a clean palette on which you can then build upon.

Now that your home is clean, it is time to think about color. If you are moving furniture from your previous home into your new one, you already have something to work from. Take a good look around your home.

Now is the time to add a fresh coat of paint to truly claim the space. Nothing can freshen up a home like a new coat of paint. Choosing colors does not need to be too difficult either. Stay with your tastes and go with complimentary colors. Don't be afraid of bold color either.

A splash of color here and there will go a long way to add excitement and character to your home. Interested in adding a bit of warm energy in your kitchen? Try using a splash of vibrant red on an accent wall.

Would you like your bathroom to send cool waves of serenity? Try a tranquil shade of aqua blue. Regardless of your choices, once the home has been painted, you will feel more connected to it.

Of course, you will have to decide whether to do it yourself or hire painters. This boils down to comfort and cost and every new homeowner needs to decide which way to proceed. But it is certain that painting your home can be one of the fastest ways to claim your new living space.

Now that your home is clean and painted, it is time to add some accents. Adding a few air filtering plants is a wonderful way to add some nature and fresh air to your home. A throw pillow here and there can add some spice to your living room.

A well placed and color coordinated vase can add interest to an empty space. Personal photos on the mantle add a great touch of family and friends to your home.

These touches can be small, inexpensive, and easy but speak volumes about your personality and all those who live in your home. This part can be done relatively quickly. And the beauty of adding these touches is that you can change them over time.

By cleaning, painting, and accessorizing your newly purchased home, you will quickly claim your space, feel at home, and begin to enjoy living in your new abode. Whether you moved down the block or across the country, these quick and easy steps will glide you into your home for as many years as you desire.

Chapter 2 - The Minimalist Diet Plan

Moving into a previously owned home can be a bit jarring. You are now moving into a structure that absorbed the character of the previous owners. Depending on whom you purchased the home from, you will have a great deal of work to do before the home will feel like yours. Be careful! Many new home owners begin to list all the things they would like to alter in their newly acquired home.

Not only is this expensive, it is mentally exhausting. Rather than take on the entire home, you need to prioritize. Here are some simple and relatively inexpensive things to do to make that home feel like yours in no time.

First and foremost, give the house a good top to bottom scrubbing. The previous homeowners may have been lovely people, but chances are good that the home was neglected a bit in the cleanliness department. Fixtures, floors, refrigerator, lint screens of dryers, stairs, and carpets should all get your tender loving care.

Tiles in the kitchen may need some extra attention, particularly the grout. Use a simple cleaner and add some non-chlorinated bleach alternative to warm water. Let it soak on your grout and then scrub with a brush.

Wipe, dry, and repeat until that tile looks like new! Windows will need to wiped, carpets may have to be steamed, and floors will need to be mopped. It will take much energy and sweat, but the result will be a sparkling clean home - a clean palette on which you can then build upon.

Patricia Foster

Now that your home is clean, it is time to think about color. If you are moving furniture from your previous home into your new one, you already have something to work from. Take a good look around your home. Now is the time to add a fresh coat of paint to truly claim the space.

Nothing can freshen up a home like a new coat of paint. Choosing colors does not need to be too difficult either. Stay with your tastes and go with complimentary colors. Don't be afraid of bold color either. A splash of color here and there will go a long way to add excitement and character to your home. Interested in adding a bit of warm energy in your kitchen?

Try using a splash of vibrant red on an accent wall. Would you like your bathroom to send cool waves of serenity? Try a tranquil shade of aqua blue. Regardless of your choices, once the home has been painted, you will feel more connected to it. Of course, you will have to decide whether to do it yourself or hire painters.

This boils down to comfort and cost and every new homeowner needs to decide which way to proceed. But it is certain that painting your home can be one of the fastest ways to claim your new living space.

Now that your home is clean and painted, it is time to add some accents. Adding a few air filtering plants is a wonderful way to add some nature and fresh air to your home. A throw pillow here and there can add some spice to your living room.

A well placed and color coordinated vase can add interest to an empty space. Personal photos on the mantle add a great touch of family and friends to your home.

These touches can be small, inexpensive, and easy but speak volumes about your personality and all those who live in your

Minimalist Living for Peace of Mind

home. This part can be done relatively quickly. And the beauty of adding these touches is that you can change them over time.

By cleaning, painting, and accessorizing your newly purchased home, you will quickly claim your space, feel at home, and begin to enjoy living in your new abode. Whether you moved down the block or across the country, these quick and easy steps will glide you into your home for as many years as you desire.

Chapter 3- Making The Transition To the Minimalist Lifestyle

Everyone faces bumps in his or her financial road at some point in life, but today's unemployment statistics make it clear the financial bumps are as numerous as gopher holes on the prairie and shared by many. One big difference between those who will sink during economic upheavals and those who survive is that survivors are able to distinguish between "wants" and "needs." This ability allows them to restructure their lives and make prudent purchasing decisions.

The list of *"needs"* basic to human survival includes food, shelter, and clothing. Add "transportation" to that list, because most communities now are built with shopping or employment opportunities surrounding residential areas.

"*Shelter*" would include utilities; running water is essential, heat is a must in the Dakotas, Minnesota and New England, and air conditioning is necessary in places such as Texas or Arizona. Beyond these items, everything else is a "*want*." Cable television, high speed internet, smart phones, magazine and newspaper subscriptions and a membership to the gym or country club are luxuries. So is dining out, even if it's at Mickey D's.

When income is scarce and there is no relief in the immediate future, these nonessentials should be the first to go. Before the Blackberry, people survived using a basic landline telephone. Entertainment is available for free at the local library; most libraries lend movies, audio books, e-books and music in addition to books and magazines.

Even within the "*need*" category, there are options that are economical and options that demand more resources. For example, a filling, nutritious meal can be produced using ground beef and pasta as the primary ingredients.

The same meal comes in a variety of pre-packaged forms at nearly twice the cost of making it from scratch. Chicken, fish, beans and peanut butter are not only less expensive protein sources than are beef and pork, but they are healthier choices as well.

For the past ten years, nutritionists and physicians have been advocating a diet lower in animal protein; economics may make this a reality for more Americans, which may inadvertently lead to lower health care costs and a better quality of life later on.

For a low-cost treat, try baking cookies, making popcorn or whipping up some old-fashioned desserts like bread pudding, rice pudding or baked apples. "Scratch" cooking and baking aren't as difficult or as time consuming as some people imagine them to be, and the cost differences between "homemade" and "packaged" adds up to some nice savings over time.

Compulsive shoppers are the frugal clothes buyer's best friends. Look through any consignment store or Goodwill store, and designer labels that are in nearly mint-condition abound. Purchase a classic style rather than something that is "so-2011" and no one will know that it was purchased "gently used."

As for transportation, driving a beater (*paid for with cash*), taking the bus, riding a bicycle or walking may not enhance one's aura of "cool," but these options do allow a person to get out from under the oppression of a car loan.

Using public transportation, walking or biking also eliminates the need for auto insurance, and that can eliminate an expense of a few hundred dollars a month. In addition, walking or biking daily improves both physical and mental health; 45 minutes of regular, rhythmic movement daily reduces stress, tones muscles and burns calories.

De-stressing when economic pressures close in offsets the human tendency to self-medicate in other, more destructive, ways; during the past two years, alcohol and cigarette sales have risen.

Finally, expenses related to home ownership may be the largest monthly outlays in the budget. While it may be tempting to stop paying for insurance or be late with utility payments, doing so would invite disaster. Utility companies are the first to report late payments to credit bureaus, and going without homeowner's insurance may violate terms written into a mortgage.

Utility companies do try to accommodate hardship situations; if they are called before non-payment or late payments become an issue, they may allow deferred payments, develop a budget-billing plan, or make other arrangements so that there won't be a shutoff later. Some utility companies offer a variety of service plans with competitive rates that would be more suitable. Ask for the best plan for your situation.

Unemployment and other financial hardships are temporary situations so this list of lifestyle changes can also be temporary. However, if they are maintained when finances improve, a frugal lifestyle can transform what was a pay-check-to-pay-check existence into a wealth-building powerhouse life.

Chapter 4 - Simple Frugal and Minimalist Tactics

We are all well aware of the skyrocketing costs of living. Groceries, utilities, taxes and rent are all climbing. Saving money by updating and replacing inefficient appliances and home products can be costly. Many companies offer products that can save us thousands of dollars a year.

However, many of these products cost many thousands of dollars. For a lot of us, those funds are not available to invest in money saving improvements. There are still a number of ways that you can save significantly and make a real dent in the chasm between take home pay and monthly bills.

Laundry

Look at the way you care for the laundry and your family's habits. There may be ways to conserve energy and save yourself some work at the same time. Is it possible to wear an item more than once? Can the jeans worn on Tuesday be worn on Wednesday as well? Perhaps they can be rotated and worn on Thursday.

If an outfit is tried on and rejected, is it discarded on the floor only to end up in the laundry basket?

Are bathroom towels hung up to dry and used multiple times? How often are the bed sheets changed?

Extend the use of items between laundering to save money.

Minimalist Living for Peace of Mind

If you can reduce the number of loads of laundry you do each week, you have saved money on several fronts. The amount of water used for a load of laundry can vary greatly.

If you wash a full load, each load not done can save approx. 47 gallons of water. You are saving on the amount of laundry detergent and fabric softener used and the electricity or gas required to wash and dry those clothes.

Bathroom Activities

Consider installing water restrictor devices on your water faucets. Purchase heads for both showers and sink faucets at hardware stores and home improvement centers.

There are showerheads that use only 1.5-GPM, as opposed to a normal head that uses as much as 4-GPM. The starting price for this device is around $10.50.

This small investment is worth a lot in terms of annual savings. A standard 4- GPM bathroom sink faucet can be replaced with a low-flow model that uses only 1.5-GPM. This cost as little as $2.50, so it is a very affordable change you can make.

Have a timer in the bathroom to help the family reduce the time they spend in the shower. The five-minute challenge is fun for the kids and reminds adults not to linger.

A ten-minute shower using 4-GPM is 40 gallons of water; a five-minute shower using 4-GPM is 20 gallons. That same 5 minutes using a 1.5-GPM restrictor is only 7.5 gallons of water.

Add a water displacement device to your toilet. A toilet typically uses approximately four gallons of water for each flush. Rather than buying a device, use a half-gallon milk bottle. Fill part way with gravel for weight, then fill the remainder with water and cap it. Carefully place it in the toilet tank, making sure that it does not interfere with the flushing mechanism.

This will save one half gallon of water every time the toilet is flushed. The average person uses the toilet 5 times a day. For a family of five, that can be a savings of 350 gallons of water each month or over 4000 gallons annually. If your toilet leaks, replace the flapper with one that properly seals for under $2.00.

Teach the family to leave the water off when brushing teeth. Wet the brush, turn off the water, apply the toothpaste, and brush. When it is time to rinse, then turn on the faucet. This small act adds up to big savings, especially if the faucet has a low-flow adapter attached to it.

In The Kitchen

Make sure the dishwasher is full before running it. Do not load it with a few huge pans or skillets. Wash those by hand and fill the dishwasher with dinnerware and glasses. When you wash those oversized pots and pans, use one as a dish pan and do not let the water continue to run. Wash them all and then rinse them.

Add a low-flow water restrictor to your kitchen faucet. If your faucet uses 4-GPM, the restrictor will reduce that to as little as 1.5-GPM. If you peel your vegetables in the sink, rinse them with water and then turn off the faucet.

Do not run the water while peeling and cutting them. When they are all cut and peeled, rinse them all at one time.

Conserving water helps the environment and cuts utility costs. Families can make significant savings by developing new habits around the house.

Minimalist Living for Peace of Mind

None of these is difficult or expensive and is easily accomplished without special tools or mechanical knowledge. Frugal living is not deprivation. It is learning to live smarter and making the most of the resources available.

Chapter 5 - Being Minimalist At The Office

Could your office's appearance be contributing to your work-related stress? Whether it's from mountains of clutter or a lack of natural light, how your workspace looks can impact how you feel when you're in it.

Working in a stressful space can make work a depressing and frustrating experience, leading to lower productivity and a lack of fulfillment in your career.

Improving the look of your office surroundings can take your workplace from stressful to serene in no time. Here are some tips to help you spruce up your space:

Find a place for everything. If you have files and paperwork strewn across the office or stacked on every possible surface, it's time to find a more sensible solution. Invest in some storage equipment to fill your needs.

Filing cabinets, in-boxes and shelving units can all go a long way in making your non-digital data more accessible. Start small if you're not sure how much equipment you need, but make baby steps towards a better-organized workplace.

Put everything in its place. As you acquire storage equipment, use it! Start cutting through the clutter and filing things in their appropriate places. The sooner you devise an organization system, the sooner it'll become second nature. Start now, before your mess gets even more out of hand. Once everything is filed away, your office will immediately look much more pleasant and manageable.

Keep it clean. Clutter isn't the only culprit dirtying up your office. Dirt, dust, and garbage may also be contributing to an uncomfortable work environment. Unless you plan on putting vermin on the payroll, take the time to keep your office clean.

Dust and disinfect regularly. Vacuum the carpet as well as any other fabrics in the office, such as padded cubicle walls. Deal with food garbage immediately. Resolve to never let your garbage can overflow again.

Play with color. Is your office done up in boring beige? Maybe a new color is what you need to spruce up your space. Bright, light colors such as baby blue and yellow have a calming and mood-enhancing effect. If you're unable to paint, add some colorful artwork or even just some interesting magazine clippings.

Tack up pictures that transport you to a happier place if that's what it takes, but make sure you have something pleasant to look at.

Rethink your floor plan. Does your office's layout make sense? If yours is the closest desk to the door but visitors have to walk around 4 other people to get to you, something's wrong.

Make sure that your office is accessible, both to employees and to potential visitors. A well-designed floor plan will make it much easier to navigate your workspace, eliminating one more source of unnecessary stress.

Let the sun shine in. If you rely solely on artificial lights, think about letting some real sun in. Natural sunlight is known to improve happiness, and the lack of it can cause serious psychological issues such as seasonal affective disorder (SAD).

If your office doesn't have enough windows for sufficient natural sunlight, try to adjust your current lighting to be more appealing. Try brighter light bulbs, or add task lighting if your office is too dim.

Go for comfort. Physical stress in the workplace is often due to uncomfortable working conditions. Take the time to adjust your chair for proper height and lumbar support. Make sure you're not straining to reach your keyboard or mouse.

Walk around the office regularly, or just get up to stretch. Reduce eye strain by adjusting your monitor's tilt and brightness, and by looking away from the screen every so often. Giving your eyes a break will help keep you from feeling drowsy or getting headaches from staring at the monitor for too long.

Provide nourishment. If you've got a break room full of takeout menus and junk-filled vending machines, think about the unhappiness that comes with a poor diet.

We often turn to poor food choices when we're feeling stressed, but eating poorly can also cause people additional stress and self-consciousness about their appearance. Take that stress out of the equation by stocking your lunch space with fresh, healthy foods. Replacing the junk food with fruit, nuts and whole grain foods will help keep your employees making choices they can be proud of.

Don't forget fun! If your workplace is boring 100% of the time, your employees will feel like they're wearing a backpack full of bricks. Let loose once in a while! Play upbeat music throughout the work day to help keep people moving.

Offer contests or incentives to honor and encourage outstanding work. Encourage casual Fridays or a more relaxed dress code. Find a way to help your employees relax without sacrificing the quality of their work.

By making your office an attractive, fun place to work, stress levels will go down while productivity goes up. Who says you can't love what you do for a living?

Chapter 6- From The Office To The Home With Minimalism

If you feel a need to spruce up your bedroom, but don't think you have the money to do it, take heart: there are many inexpensive ways to make a room look better with just a little hard work and creativity. Below are several different options to consider. Mix and match the ones that fit your circumstances, and have a blast.

1) Rearrange the furniture. This is a fairly labour-intensive proposition, but it's also totally free; no need to buy new stuff, just rearrange what you already have for a completely new look. This step should only be done with the help of friends or spouse; don't try to do it on your own.

2) Change out the knick-knacks. Have you been looking at the same "dust collectors" on your shelves for years? It may be time to switch them out. Change them out with knick-knacks from another room if you don't want to get rid of them, or pass them along to someone else and find new ones at thrift stores and yard sales.

This can become expensive very quickly (*five dollar items add up fast*), but if you're careful, it doesn't have to be. Just set yourself a "yard sale budget" and stick to it carefully.

3) Change out the bedclothes. This can be as expensive as buying a completely new bedroom set, or as cheap as covering the bed with a sheet that complements your current pillowcases. Also, change your sheets once a week. Sleeping on fresh sheets goes a long way towards improving your outlook on life.

4) Grab a throw rug. You can buy one for the bedroom if you have plenty of money…but if you don't, find one somewhere else in your house and move it. (If you have friends who are getting rid of a good, usable throw rug, don't be ashamed to ask if you can have it.

Offer to exchange something you're getting rid of if you don't want to take without giving something in return.

5) Change the curtains. If you have some skill with sewing, you can make your own. Otherwise, consider purchasing them. If you buy simple curtains, they need not be expensive, and they can add a whole new look to a room.

6) Fresh flowers. If you have a garden, picking a few fresh flowers and putting them in vases can perk up a room no end. Don't buy flowers if you don't have them fresh, however; flowers in general are either free or incredibly expensive, and not worth buying.

7) Switch furniture with other rooms. Similar to switching out knick-knacks and throw rugs, sometimes just changing out a couple of pieces of furniture, such as chairs or small shelving units, with pieces from another room, can really make a difference in a room.

The same goes for lamps or desk lights; if you can move it, consider changing it out with something similar from a different room.

8) Clean up. Cheap but labour-intensive, DE cluttering can go a long way towards changing the feel of a room. Working fifteen or twenty minutes at a time, either find a home for each item in your room, or else get rid of it.

9) Add or remove a painting. Small but pretty prints can be purchased for as little as $10 or $15, or sometimes even as little as $5, and adding one to your room can improve the overall feel of the room.

Alternately, if you feel like your room is cluttered and crowded, you may want to consider removing any paintings you currently have on your walls.

Allowing a little empty space on your walls can keep you from feeling so overwhelmed all the time. If you tend to stress out over little things, try clearing off your walls. You might be surprised by how much it helps.

10) Finally, consider repainting your walls. This is perhaps the most expensive suggestion of all those listed here, and not something to rush into. Before painting your walls, try wiping them with a damp rag to remove any accumulated dirt (*wipe a small and inconspicuous section first, to make sure the walls are washable*!), and get any cobwebs out of the corners.

Sometimes this will add enough pep to the room that painting the walls won't be necessary. However, if your walls are very dirty, dingy, and stained or scuffed, it may be worth saving up and putting a single coat of the same color over the walls to freshen the room up.

Changing the color of the walls is much more difficult and more expensive, and doesn't really belong in an article on inexpensive decorating solutions. But adding a fresh coat of paint can make a huge difference.

Chapter 7 - Minimalism For Students

Higher education is, unfortunately, expensive. Tuition, accommodation, books, and other expenses can quickly eat away at any student or parents' budget.

Luckily, there are ways in which to ease the financial burden that college and university may place on a person. Here are ten tips which every student should know to make things a bit easier on both the pocket and on the bank account.

1. Student surveys and experiments – Many colleges and university have vibrant psychology departments, where students are often paid for taking part in surveys and experiments. These experiments are extremely safe, as there are often stringent safety requirements that must be adhered to. Although the payment is usually relatively small, a couple hours of experiments per week can quickly add up into a decent amount of money.

2. Buy second hand items - There are certain items that can be bought second hand which will save students a huge amount of money. Many second hand books for courses will be available, allowing students to save massive amounts on expensive course materials. Many other items, such as chairs, desks or other furniture, can be bought in good condition second hand, both in local shops and stores or online.

3. Re Sell – On the flip side of the coin, students can easily sell items that they may no longer need. Books are usually only good for one semester, and when moving house students may choose to sell unwanted or unnecessary furniture. These articles can quickly turn into a goldmine due to the available market of future incoming students.

4. Ask about scholarship, bursaries and grants that the university offers – Often, due to academic performance or financial need, students may qualify for scholarships, bursaries or grants that they may not even know about.

These can represent either significant financial savings or direct payments which will assist in easing the financial squeeze. It is important to check with the school's relevant financial assistance department to see if the student qualifies for any sort of financial assistance or relief.

5. Student employment – Many schools have a wide variety of jobs available, from work in shops, computer labs, or secretarial type work. These schools will usually advertise these jobs to the students first on the inter-campus websites, allowing them first preference to these jobs, so it is important to keep up to date with these websites to know if and when any job postings may become available.

6. Student cards – Students generally are given discounts at a number of locations, both locally and further afield. Using a student card to save 5% or 10% on purchases will definitely add up in the long run.

7. Insurance - Having insurance is one not so obvious way to save money as a student. Insuring valuable, but necessary goods is a great way to prevent further expense in case they get damaged or stolen. This is especially true for electronic items such as laptops and mobile phones, which can be easily damaged and are also frequent targets for theft.

Having insurance ensures that in cases of unfortunate damage or loss, the student has a means of recovering the item without spending little or any extra.

8. Budget – Frequently, when students go to university is the first time that they are financially on their own. Tasks such as buying food, paying for groceries or rent are novel to them.

As a result, they do not have an idea of how much money to spend, and often end up finding themselves in deep trouble when their bank accounts run dry. Having a budget ensures that the student will be far more knowledgeable about the money being spent and earned, reducing the likelihood of financial issues.

9. Save – On those occasions where students actually have a surplus of funds, they regularly end up spending this money on disposable or unnecessary items. While there is need for recreational spending, a portion of any *"extra"* money should be put into a dedicated savings account for emergency purposes, rainy days, or just used as a start to good spending habits.

10. Smart Shopping – Simple tricks like buying budget brands instead of premium, or shopping at value supermarkets can easily save hundreds a year. It is a great idea to figure out what items are frequently purchased, and then compare these prices with other supermarkets in the area. The internet is also a fantastic resource, as many items can easily be compared and purchased online.

Chapter 8 - Tips For The Minimalist Traveler

Family summer vacations are a tradition for many across the country, and stories of those trips are staples in the *"What I Did on Summer Vacation"* essays on the first day of school. But in these tough economic times, many families are making a hard realization; a vacation simply doesn't fit into the budget this year.

While for some this may seem like a harsh blow, not taking the family away on vacation doesn't have to cause misery or distress. In fact, it's possible to have just as much fun on a family "stay-cation" as on a trip away somewhere. Not to mention staying home can potentially save thousands of dollars for the average family. The trick to a successful "stay-cation" is this: be creative!

Among the most popular summer vacation destinations are beaches and water parks, where families can escape the summer heat in cool water and exciting attractions. But beach vacation rentals and water park admissions costs can be astronomical, especially for families of four and more.

For water-loving families, a home vacation can be fun for everyone without sacrificing any of the excitement water parks offer. Families who wish to build at home water parks need to do their homework; watch sale papers and ads for the very lowest prices on things like kiddie or inflatable pools, slip-n-slides, and sprinklers. After these are purchased at rock bottom prices, it's up to family creativity to find fun ways to put them all together. Handy family members can even build water attractions from PVC pipe, plumbing connectors and hoses. Though a family's water bill will go up while supporting these mini water parks, the cost is insignificant when compared to the expense of a beach or water park vacation.

Patricia Foster

For those families that aren't overly interested in water fun, "stay-cations," there are still options for fun at home. Summer is the perfect time to explore nature, and get to know the world around us with our families. But many families looking for a true "stay-cation" aren't looking to take an actual camping trip with all the preparation and supplies those excursions call for. Those families need fear not; it's easy to get the great outdoors experience for the whole family while staying right at home.

For this at-home vacation, families should use their own backyards, and the very least expensive camping gear available. A lightweight tent, a ground covering tarp, a few flashlights and sleeping pads or bags will be plenty to get any family through a home camping trip. The best part about a stay-at-home camping excursion?

All the conveniences of home are right there for a family to use, including indoor bathrooms and kitchens. Simply committing to spending the majority of a "stay-cation" outside, exploring the outdoors and stargazing, is enough to make this at-home vacation fun.

One of the great mysteries of the world is why so many people are so unfamiliar with the cities and town in which they live. Some people live their whole lives in a city or town and never experience all it has to offer. For families' intent on a summer "stay-cation," this can be a thing of the past. A great tip for anyone who wants to avoid expensive vacations but still have a great time exploring, is to explore all things local. Museums, art galleries, parks and zoos; even train depots, historical homes and posh restaurants are hometown destinations too many people overlook.

Often, area attractions will offer discounts for locals who can provide proof of residence, often with simply a driver's license. For even deeper discounts, "stay-cationers" can sign up for online coupon sites like Groupon. Not only is this a great way for families

Minimalist Living for Peace of Mind

to save hard-earned money, it also offers the opportunity for anyone to get to know their hometown.

Family summer vacations are, of course, a well-loved tradition, and certainly will not fade away into the sunset anytime soon. But for families who need a less expensive alternative, nothing beats a family "stay-cation" for frugal fun and adventure. With a little creativity, and lots of good spirit, a stay-home vacation can provide just as much family fun as the most expensive vacation.

Patricia Foster

Chapter 9- Back To Decorating Your Minimalist Style Home

In today's economic climate many people are on tight budgets, making redecorating one of the last things on their to do lists. Expensive home decor and furnishings seem out of reach when energy and food costs are skyrocketing. However, with a little creativity and patience, it is possible to find quality decor to fit any budget.

Whether you want to completely redecorate your home or buy a few items, here are *5 ideas for finding great decor* and furnishings on a tight budget.

1. Family and Friends: People will hold onto all sorts of things they don't need or want because of sentimental reasons. Your family and friends have probably abandoned all sorts of unwanted goodies in their attics and garages. So don't be shy, let everyone know you are looking for furniture and home accessories for a redecorating project. You may be surprised who jumps at the chance to give Grandma's antique picture frame or coffee table to a good home. With friends and family you may just get your furnishings at the best price. Free.

2. Estate Sales: These 2 to 3 day sale events are great resources for finding quality furniture and home goods that may otherwise be out of financial reach. There are many websites that list local estate sales that provide photographs, logistics, and merchandise details. This makes it easier to find estate sales that fit not just your budget, but your decorating tastes as well. The most popular pieces sell first, so if you want that mid-century buffet, be one of the first in the door. If you want the best prices, go to the sale on the last day because the merchandise is usually marked down 50% or more. Don't forget to carry cash, because many estate sales do not accept credit cards or checks. Even those that do, cash is still king and having it may give you the upper hand while negotiating.

3. Craigslist: This online bulletin board is one of the best resources available for redecorating on a budget. In the privacy of your own home you can search through a variety of furnishings until you find that one must-have piece, or you can search for a particular item within a specific price range. For the most part, sellers operate on a cash and carry basis, but some will even deliver larger items for a small fee. Craigslist is a great site to find brand name, vintage, and one of a kind home decor.

4. Free cycling and Swapping: Many neighborhoods now have online groups and bulletin boards dedicated to swapping and free cycling. For instance, if you have a desk taking up valuable space, but need a decent bookcase, swapping is the perfect solution. Swapping is becoming increasingly popular making it easier to swap for top of the line items.

If swapping is not for you, research community bulletin boards like free cycle, where you can pick-up anything from a crystal punch bowl to brand new rolls of wallpaper. However, you have to be quick, claiming these items are on a first come first serve basis.

5. Going out of Business Sales: Unfortunately many home furnishing stores and design shops are either going out of business or closing low-performing stores. Going out of business sales give you the opportunity to purchase name brand and high-end home goods at deeply discounted prices.

To make as much money as possible, these stores usually discount their merchandise gradually over the course of a few months. If you can, wait until the final two or three weeks of the sale to take advantage of the final price slashing.

Not only can you get brand new furnishings and decor at a fraction of their original cost, you can also get floor models, samples, and display-only items for unbelievably cheap.

You do not have to sacrifice design or quality when shopping for home decor and furnishings on a tight budget. With a little time and research it is possible to get great things at great prices. So go ahead, put redecorating back at the top of your to do list.

About the Author

Patricia Foster is a true believer in the tenets of minimalism. She was once living in a world where she had to have more than she needed to feel as if she was achieving some goal or was using her earnings to show how much she had. She had the gaudiest house and the fanciest car she could afford.

One day she simply came to the realization that she really was stressing herself out more than anything else when she opted to put herself in debt to get all of these things.

This is what led Patricia to change and this is what led her to share her journey with others and show them that nothing is wrong with minimalism.